HAL•LEONARD INSTRUMENTAL PLAY-ALONG

AUDIO ACCESS INCLUDED

PLAYBACK+
Speed • Pitch • Balance • Loop

TROMBONE

THE GREATEST SHOWMAN

Audio Arrangements by Peter Deneff

To access audio visit:
www.halleonard.com/mylibrary

Enter Code
7206-3675-5005-7082

ISBN 978-1-5400-2846-4

HAL•LEONARD®

7777 W. BLUEMOUND RD. P.O. BOX 13819 MILWAUKEE, WI 53213

In Australia Contact:
Hal Leonard Australia Pty. Ltd.
4 Lentara Court
Cheltenham, Victoria, 3192 Australia
Email: ausadmin@halleonard.com.au

Visit Hal Leonard Online at
www.halleonard.com

COME ALIVE

TROMBONE

Words and Music by BENJ PASEK
and JUSTIN PAUL

FROM NOW ON

TROMBONE

Words and Music by BENJ PASEK
and JUSTIN PAUL

THE GREATEST SHOW

TROMBONE

Words and Music by BENJ PASEK,
JUSTIN PAUL and RYAN LEWIS

A MILLION DREAMS

TROMBONE

Words and Music by BENJ PASEK
and JUSTIN PAUL

NEVER ENOUGH

TROMBONE

Words and Music by BENJ PASEK
and JUSTIN PAUL

THE OTHER SIDE

TROMBONE

Words and Music by BENJ PASEK
and JUSTIN PAUL

REWRITE THE STARS

TROMBONE

Words and Music by BENJ PASEK
and JUSTIN PAUL

THIS IS ME

TROMBONE

Words and Music by BENJ PASEK
and JUSTIN PAUL

TIGHTROPE

TROMBONE

Words and Music by BENJ PASEK
and JUSTIN PAUL